HOW TO REPAIR LEATHER BAGS
GUIDE FOR BEGINNERS

Ultimate beginners guide on how to repair leather bags, techniques while choosing a calfskin pack and manual for fixing enormous breaks in cowhide sacks

Table of Contents

CHAPTER ONE

INTRODUCTION

The best material for wallets, sacks, and packs is calfskin. Strength, ludicrous style, and crazy style are completely combined in it. Be that as it may, regardless of its solidarity, cowhide trim is helpless to harm, so I've furnished you with this apparatus for fixing your calfskin adornments.

One of the most amazing elements of calfskin sacks is the manner by which they adjust to your developments. They are a solitary piece with specific qualities. Your cowhide sack can change into a fortune for your approaching age's loved ones with a touch of delicate love and care. One of the privileged insights is the means by which to fix a harmed calfskin sack. In the case of nothing else works, you ought to have the option to fix the issue yourself at home or with the assistance of an expert on the off chance that the issue is more serious. The most effective way to fix scratches on wallets, packs, and sacks made of cowhide Scratches are the most well-known sort of harm, and as your pack progresses in years, you could have to spend more the means to fix broken calfskin. You could possibly cover the scratches with a cowhide tone in the event that the scratches aren't really awful. For extra unbelievable scratches, brief thought is run of the mill. Right when let be, they could make and tear the cowhide. A calfskin fix unit is expected for these to be fixed. Most calfskin fix units use grain paper, a power executes, and a liquid paste for two or three tones. Apply the treatment to the scratch on various occasions with a liquid significant that exactly matches the shade of your calfskin wallet, handbag, or pack. It very well may be useful for you to incorporate a toothpick for this. The subsequent stage is to cover the scratch with grain paper, which is undoubtedly the grain of your article. The power instrument is then used to warm the grain paper. From that point forward, the paste should shape a bond with the external layer of the cowhide. At long last, permit it to cool.

Heading for the most effective way to fix openings: Use calfskin cleaner to completely clean your wallet, purse, or sack, then, at that point, let it dry. This is tremendous when you consider that any oil or soil at a shallow level could keep the paste from being impeccably found. The messed up defect in the cowhide should be loaded up with the glue. It is conceivable that you will anticipate that somebody should hold the cowhide set up while you apply the paste. Utilizing a piece of fine sandpaper, eliminate any overabundance buildup once the glue has dried. You totally should partake in intense consideration practice while doing this; The calfskin could be scratched surprisingly. Following playing out a second cleaning with a cowhide cleaner, permit the locale to dry to guarantee that each overabundance stick has been killed.

TIPS FOR DIY FIXING HOW TO FIX YOUR STUFF

Knowing how to fix your stuff can be helpful while you're fanning out and attempting to track down a few tears in your pack. You could correspondingly need to manage several torn edges in your pack after you travel. Despite the fact that incredible brands have their own help and fix groups, assuming you have a little satchel, you ought to deal with its upkeep all alone.

Coming up next are instances serious areas of strength for of:

Tip 1: Vinyl and other normal materials can be stuck to surfaces with concrete made explicitly for vinyl. You can get this at dress fix stores. The expense of supplanting the sack isn't especially high. Fundamentally, you can utilize the harmed region by eliminating a piece of cement. It seems to be fixing a rooftop opening.

Tip 2: You can utilize both vinyl fix and cement to fix a huge tear that can't be really fixed with concrete. Cut the vinyl fix into a size that is fitting for the tear you are fixing. Associate it under the harmed region. Seal the region by applying the vinyl concrete.

Tip 3: You can attempt a methodology like tip 2 in the event that your cowhide gear has a critical tear or tear. To apply cowhide fix to the harmed region, cut it to the fitting size. Ensure the calfskin is a similar grouping and surface for a strong appearance. Set up it with a surface stick. This is open from the surface store.

Tip 4: Open the metal pack or hard-sized metal sack that has blemishes on it and utilize a durable item like a block of wood to hammer out the carving inside. You can take a stab at covering the wood with a surface to try not to initially scratch the metal.

Tip 5: most of broken handles are hard to fix. You ought to dispose of it. Buy a substitution handle. Dispose of the sack's past handle. Conceivable you'll have to eliminate lines or delivery screws. Add the unparalleled handle after you have taken out the past handle. Supplant the handle plan's bolt with one that is almost indistinguishable. With the expectation that it will cover your effects, sew a surface like them onto the sack.

Tip 6: Take a stab at applying a limited quantity of a smooth substance, like a manufactured, to assist the stuck zipper with relaxing prior to endeavoring to fix it. Assuming a ton of surface is trapped in the zipper, pry it off to open the one that is stuck. You ought to have it supplanted immediately assuming that you believe it's phony, which you ought to. On the off chance that the pack has a fragile surface, basically eliminate the zipper joint and buy a substitution zipper of a similar length and mix. Match the arrangements to the better one. For things that come in hard cases, you ought to recruit a specialist to fix the zipper.

CHAPTER TWO

A COUPLE OF TIPS TO ASSIST WITH PICKING THE SACK

What is the Most Well known Item for Ladies? Is it the wonderful dress, the fragrance, or the snazzy shoes? No, I think the most revered item for me is the pack. It could rejuvenate your whole dress, yet it could likewise mirror your own style. Anyway, how to pick the suitable sack for ourselves? Whether or not you pick a tote or a Rucksack Pack, picking the right sack is significant data. I could get a kick out of the chance to offer a few pointers to the people who are experiencing issues choosing a sensible sack.

The most notable material of today is cow calfskin; In any case, the sheepskin is the most ideal choice. The lines of the sheepskin are fine and firmly woven, and the sheepskin has both magnificence and strength. Likewise, these sorts of sacks are agreeable to hold and have a dazzling curve.

The patent cowhide and chamois calfskin are additionally very notable as of late. Approached the patent calfskin, it is genuinely hard to save in decent shape for the chamois cowhide, and the patent calfskin is more sleek and significant. Subsequently, while going with your choices, you ought to consider your choices as a whole.

Plan while the backpack pack is the style of the stylish small kid, the shoulder sack is ordinarily a kind of refined style that is fitting for created women. Moreover, the direct plan of the advantageous pack makes it the most ideal choice for proficient ladies. The granting pack to metallic extra isn't simply the most ideal choice for clean ladies yet in addition tends to their personality.

TECHNIQUE WHILE CHOOSING A CALFSKIN PACK

The whole creature, as well as the assortment, lines, and belt length, ought to be thought about immediately. The plan, zipper, wrinkle crossing, and covering of the sack ought to likewise be thought about. You can press the kink crossing to check whether there is some missed join. Besides, we accept that understand several expert hypotheses ought to pick the prominent brand. To buy them, I propose you go to the large store with the best evaluating. Likewise, you truly need to keep them with everything looking great as your direction.

Style of the dress Assuming you are a young lady who is keen on design and is intending to wear a notable assortment dress, you ought to pick a sack that works out positively for your dress. Expecting that you appreciate wearing a basic assortment dress; I believe that the stunning travel bag is the most ideal decision for you. In the event that you like to wear shirts or game suits, I think a backpack pack made of sailcloth or plastic would be better for you.

Ability while style and point of view are fundamental while choosing a handbag, their ability ought not be ignored. Past the bag is a minuscule pocket; Keeping a couple of little things close by is very useful. Also, there are some little sack, which you can use to keep changes, keys and another extra thing. The housewife will view it as exceptionally unwinding to utilize. Today, we partake throughout everyday life. When Christmas Day shows up, would you say you are ready to send a present to your friends and family or something for yourself? Alright, how about we stop here; I want to go get a few gifts for my loved ones. Of cause, I will pick a rucksack for my Christmas business. Set up a present for your kid and companions to buy a pack or knapsack for work.

STYLE GUIDANCE FOR MEN

How to Really focus on Your Cowhide Frill A great deal of men truly like calfskin extras since they can cause an outfit to seem more appealing and offer something more significant. Cowhide sacks, for example, PC packs, cowhide belts, calfskin shoes, and belts are extremely normal. In any case, it is vital for deal with cowhide gear while buying it. Nothing looks more horrendous than dry, broke, old-and-not-oversaw cowhide ribbon.

METHOD FOR DEALING WITH YOUR COWHIDE GEAR

1. Not long after you purchase another calfskin thing (or not long after somebody gives you one as a gift) apply a grand cowhide cream/conditioner. Reapply around once or twice a year to help with water check and keep an eye on the cowhide. Cream or conditioner should be applied with a material that is light and free of buildup. Rub a minuscule proportion of the cream or conditioner into the texture before applying it to the calfskin thing in

minimal indirect developments (remember how in the Karate Young person movie he expected to "wax on, wax off. It is essential to use a small amount and then apply it with the utmost care, scouring and polishing it in. Since the calfskin won't absorb excess use, basically eliminate any excess.

2. If a cowhide item gets wet, it should dry naturally in the air and away from heat sources. To speed up drying, do not place your calfskin gloves on a radiator; to speed up the drying of your cowhide shoes, don't use a hair dryer. When the cowhide is nearly dry, apply a small amount of calfskin cream or conditioner to restore adaptability.

3. You should never use mink oil or any other animal fat on your calfskin because it will obscure it, regardless of what anyone else says to you. Other than that, it can turn your calfskin spoiled, making the sewing and the cowhide decay.

4. Tissue paper should be full into void cowhide sacks for limit. As a result, they'll stay in shape.

5. Boots and cowhide shoes should be stored in shoe trees. If you don't have shoe trees, stuff tissue paper inside the shoes or boots to keep them in their original shape.

6. Clean smooth calfskin surfaces with a delicate, clammy cloth or material. Avoid

anything containing liquor. If your cowhide item is too grimy for water alone, give Neutrogena Facial Cleanser a try (a similar product can be found in the pharmacy's facial care aisle, but not the peeling kind). This puts a lot of pressure on the face; along these lines, various devotees of cowhide propose it for use with calfskin.

It is essential to be aware that the cream or conditioner you use on cowhide products, shoe cleaner and other items made of calfskin can be harmful. Use them in a well-ventilated area and keep them out of reach of children. When dealing with these pieces of cowhide, try not to let your kids help.

CHAPTER THREE

INSTRUCTIONS FOR REPLACING A STRIPPING COWHIDE PACK

Calfskin sacks are renowned for their flawless appearance and timeless style. Calfskin tends to be passed down from one generation to the next in a very well-kept pack due to its high strength when cleaned and molded on a regular basis.

In any case, you should be careful about respect to its assistance and take the necessary steps not to keep your cowhide pack in a very warm, cold, or low-dampness climate. If they are not cared for over time, high-quality cowhide sacks may become fragile and begin to strip.

This comprehensive guide outlines the best ways to repair a stripping cowhide pack. You'll sort out some way to fix a broke or stripping cowhide sacks outside, edges, and internal covering. replanting the inner covering; replanting and stripping the edges; Supplanting deep cracks Before getting into the specifics, it's important to look into the most common causes of cowhide packs starting to strip and talk about several ways to prevent this from happening.

REGULAR MOTIVATIONS DRIVING WHY COWHIDE SACKS STRIP

Calfskin packs can strip because of various reasons. We've compiled a list of the most well-known ones below to help you better understand them.

Using Cleaning Methods and Products That Are Unacceptable Cleaning methods and products that contain liquor or other harsh synthetic compounds can begin to strip the cowhide. Scouring liquor is utilized as a cleaning master for calfskin, by and large, however various individuals don't comprehend that it can demolish the presence of their easy cowhide pack long haul hoping to be its mauled. We propose simply using calfskin friendly cleaning and embellishment things thusly. These fixings help the standard material last for a long time and effectively clean calfskin without harming it.

Calfskin of a Lower Quality If the cowhide in your pack is not reinforced, engineered, or of a Lower Quality, it will probably begin to strip quickly once you start using it. Pleather is a conservative choice because it is a mix of engineered and genuine calfskin. However, pleather falls short of the delicate quality and adaptability of high-grade cowhide.

In addition, unlike regular calfskin, it forms unnatural connections between the various scraps of cowhide, reducing its inherent strength. Since the material is designed to last a very long time and is extremely durable, high-quality calfskin products are much less likely to strip.

A luxury cowhide pack should be cleaned and conditioned on a regular basis to avoid the possibility of it breaking or stripping. The normal oils that keep calfskin flexible and graceful disappear over time.

If you don't apply calfskin conditioners on a regular basis, they will dry out and become fragile, which could lead to stripping and breaking. We recommend shaping your calfskin sack once every two to three months if you use it frequently. This can prevent further damage and preserve your pack's delicate appearance for a considerable amount of time.

SILLY RESTRICTION OF PACK

Calfskin is an exceptionally vulnerable material that should be dealt with appropriately to guarantee that it holds its perfect appearance and versatile feel. The low humidity conditions right after you store your calfskin pack can cause the cowhide sack to dry out and begin to strip.

To ensure that the material can be introduced to regular air, cowhide packs should be kept in a buildup sack inside a rack or storeroom with standard ventilation. You ought to in this way see that cowhide packs ought to be dealt with in a concealed locale with no fast daylight or power. When exposed to light and intensity, cowhide can break or begin to strip. This can also dry the hide out and strip it of its natural oils. If you need more information, feel free to look over our point-by-point guide on the safest way to store cowhide packs.

HOW TO REPAIR A STRIPPING CALFSKIN PACK'S INNER COVERING

An inner covering protects the sack's cowhide from accidental spills or stains from the inside. A cowhide sack's interior coating will likely begin to deteriorate if it is not properly stored or cared for. A piece of the commonplace motivations driving why cowhide linings start to strip are a consequence of low stickiness conditions or power. Additionally, the coating may occasionally become tacky, resulting in a buildup on the clinched items. We will provide you with the going with procedures for your reference in order to assist you in protecting the interior covering of your sack from additional stripping and mischief.

Choice 1: To retain the entirety of the tacky buildup, sprinkle baby powder or cornstarch into a tacky and stripping pack. Apply an unstable layer of kid powder, child powder, or cornstarch to the calfskin lining of your pack in order to accomplish this. Utilize a delicate material or cotton ball to clean the interior after allowing it to sit for a few moments. You'll notice that all of the tenacity has been removed after cleaning the excess with a different fabric.

In addition, treating a stripping sack with baby powder or cornstarch is only temporary because you must reapply the powder whenever you notice increased persistence. Additionally, if you keep things in this cowhide pack, you run the risk of spilling powder while moving it around second Choice: Nail Cleaner If the cowhide lining of your sack has completely stripped away you can use a nail cleaner to clean the entire surface. A nail polish remover containing CH3)2CO can strip cowhide and assist you in removing the covering's protective layer.

Drench cotton balls with nail clean remover and spot them inside your calfskin pack to accomplish this. After having the chance to thoroughly dispose of the stripping layer, remove the outer layer of your cowhide lining. For an impeccable finish, you may need to scrub the fixing with a sensitive toothbrush.

Assuming you truly want to keep lotions, creams, and various liquids in your calfskin sack, we don't propose this decision. This is a direct result of the bet that any startling spills will make hurt the outside cowhide and render your sack unusable. Make an effort not to use nail clean remover on the load's essential body with extraordinary care. Since CH3)2CO can be shocking to calfskin, doing so will over an extended time hurt your cowhide pack.

3rd Option: Calfskin, Surface, and Vinyl Give Using privately gained things cowhide welcoming trimmings is another technique for restoring the presence of your sack's cowhide lining. To prevent further loss of the calfskin lining, you can apply these sprinkles or liquids.

For a lasting finish, they adhere to and completely cover the calfskin. A dependable vinyl, cowhide, or surface sprinkle in an assortment that supplements the covering of your pack is normal for this decision.

Keep the item away from the zipper as you apply it to the cowhide and prop the pack open until the calfskin is dry.

Choice 4: Pass It on to an Experts Shop

On the off chance that you are uncertain about fixing your stripping cowhide load with strategies, you can return it to the principal creator or a calfskin mechanics shop to have it fixed magnificently.

Generally, makers offer answers for stripping calfskin sacks. Anyway, remember that excessive brands regularly charge pay-offs for this sort of administration. We emphatically suggest this plan if you are worried about the idea of the support and require a delayed fix.

CHAPTER FOUR

THE BEST SYSTEM FOR DEFEATING STRIPPING

At the edges of calfskin sacks is to utilize a covering near the zipper and related lashes to quit stripping. Because of wear, power, and elasticity, these regions are frail against stripping. A piece of the fixes recorded under ought to be researched.

Choice 1: Utilize an Off-The-Rack Calfskin Covering Intend To work on quality, we suggest covering the stripping edges of a calfskin sack with cowhide. It can really cover minor contortions and fix them. Apply a cowhide-obliging covering strategy with a dabber to the hurt stripping edges of your calfskin. You could have to apply extra layers of the arrangement to totally seal the calfskin and forestall further deceptive nature.

Choice 2: Use Calfskin Tape for the Event Assuming your cowhide pack's striping is too wide to even consider covering with a game plan, we suggest utilizing calfskin tape for the event. The stripping and unsteady handles of a cowhide pack can be fixed with calfskin fix tape, which has a ton of solid regions for strength. Pick a kind of tape that is sensible for the area that should be fixed (regularly dull or diminish brown). Assuming that you can't find a shade that best suits you, we suggest going with a straight plan. Prior to stripping the region, verify that the cowhide isn't wet to guarantee appropriate taking care of and to eliminate any soil or development. The tape ought to be cut utilizing the size of the stripping region, and the assistance paper ought to be applied straightforwardly to the harmed region. Ensure the tape can stretch and move with the cowhide surface when you use it. Subsequently, the upkeep will be totally unnoticeable and steady with everyday practice.

MANUAL FOR FIXING ENORMOUS BREAKS IN COWHIDE SACKS

Calfskin breaks and scratches can improve a pack's character. By the by, assuming the truth of these indications of harm is pointlessly perfect, they could become diverting and decrease the general prominence of your cowhide pack.

In the event that your calfskin sack has been broken or harmed, you ought to fix the accompanying:

• Toothpick with wet surface

• Cowhide stay with conditioner

• Cleaner cowhide Clean Your Cowhide Sack The main move toward fixing openings in your calfskin sack is to completely clean it utilizing a cowhide that is incredibly predominant. Your calfskin sack will be cleaned and treated with a unique cowhide cleaning instrument that disposes of oil, soil, development, and grime. We propose cleaning the whole pack on different occasions so all shallow stamps and breaks can be killed without any problem.

Stage 2: For bigger breaks, cautiously wind the calfskin pack to uncover them prior to applying paste. To apply the calfskin adhere to the break, put a confined sum on top of the toothpick. Give the fixing material to the calfskin so the damp surface can let any overabundance stick out.

Ensure that the significant doesn't dry on the external layer of the calfskin since this will cause the improvement to seem to have been done before. For extra fundamental breaks on your calfskin pack, go over a near cycle.

Stage 3: Condition Pack Apply a few layers of your inclined in the direction of cowhide conditioner to your calfskin pack after the glue in the breaks has totally dried to guarantee that it stays essential and flexible for quite a while.

FIX FOR SEWING AND BOLTS

The essential and side bits of cowhide sacks regularly endure harm. In the event that the sewing breaks free, it will presumably be self-evident and can be fixed by charging it or furnishing extra help with a bolt.

A business case's items collect where handles or shoulder lashes meet. Thusly, in the event that the cowhide isn't produced utilizing webbing or one more piece of calfskin, it might tear. If they are not gotten with the fitting strain, bolts could cut off. They ought to be traded out before the consolidating sewing breaks.

FIXING LOCKS AND METAL FITTINGS

A typical lock deformity happens when the hasps' springs become unendurably frail. There are sporadically blemishes in the lock instrument. Number locks are at present utilized in add cases and business cases. If all else fails, on the off chance that a lock of this sort can't be opened, it could be the consequence of reckless initiative or an unnerving absence of solidarity among the gathering. Fundamentally, a lock's external layer could offer motivation clues to clearly from now through eternity. Accordingly, the safes in the Corf assortment are encased in Palladium, guaranteeing the most elevated level of safety.

There are as of now no proper canine locks or other metal parts accessible available. Thus, while coordinating a pack, contemplating changing the fittings without opening the cover is useful.

FIX OF ZIPPERS

The goof of a zipper might be a result of an expansion of the farewell of the slider, on the off chance that it doesn't have an impact nice strain to close the teeth or little gets. Because of the way that you fundamentally need to utilize pincers to really close the opening, upkeep is vital in this present circumstance.

Expecting the zipper's webbing is torn, an assistance is hazardous. In the ongoing situation, the zipper ought to be supplanted. Basic ought to be the situation: basically open the sewing on different sides, add-on the new zipper, and reattach the sewing, which might be awkward considering the need to utilize the continuous openings. On the off chance that a pack is especially old, exchanging a zipper may not be useful contemplating how long included. The issue with the cover could be accomplished by a tore wrinkle or by a compartment that was inside tumbling off. The probability of clearing the whole cover, like an inside pack, is regularly fundamental for upkeep.

If the case is covered and the edge is exchanged, broken edges on an attache or reliable box ought to be fixed. This requires some speculation and may not be basic. The attache cases in the Corf assortment are made of aluminum shapes that are difficult to break and can be fixed assuming they are bowed.

THE END

Printed in Great Britain
by Amazon